Plug and Play Personality

By Ralph A. Morgan, Ph.D.

information. No warranties of any kind are declared or implied. Readers acknowledge that the authors do not render legal, financial, medical, or professional advice. The content within this book has been derived from various sources. Please consult a licensed professional before attempting any techniques aligned with this book.

By reading this document, the reader agrees that under no circumstances are the authors responsible for any losses, direct or indirect, that are incurred as a result of the use of the information contained within this document, including, but not limited to, errors, omissions, or inaccuracies.

No part of this publication may be reproduced or transmitted in any form or by any means, electronically or mechanically, except as permitted by law, without the copyright owner's written consent, except for brief segments quoted in a book review. The advice and strategies found within may not be suitable for some situations or is sold with the understanding that neither the authors nor the publishers are held responsible for the results curated from the advice in this book.

ISBN:

Ralph A. Morgan, Ph.D.
Biography

Ralph A. Morgan was born in Newton, New Jersey, in 1950, to Benjamin and Rozella Morgan. Benjamin was a blacksmith. Rozella was a stay-at-home mom. The family was poor, from a socio-economic perspective, but Ralph and his three siblings learned early how to work and earn money for the extra things they wanted in their lives. Ralph worked on a farm during his high school years but was able to find time to play football, wrestle, and play baseball. He was elected president of his senior class and was accepted in the U.S. Coast Guard Academy for his freshman year of college. After having a negative experience as a cadet, Ralph resigned his commission and left Connecticut for New Mexico where he was drafted in the first lottery for the Vietnam era war.

After boot camp and advanced individual training, Ralph opted to become a Special Forces soldier (Green

Beret). Upon earning his flash, he received orders for Vietnam. Ralph was assigned to a radio relay site at Khe Sanh which was overrun soon after he got there on June 4, 1971. Ralph received the Silver Star for his part in this conflict and was reassigned to a reconnaissance unit for the remainder of his tour of duty.

After returning home, Ralph attended Glassboro State College where he studied psychology to help cope with the transition back into civilian life. Upon completion of his degree, Ralph began a thirty-five year career in criminal justice that included positions as an investigator with domestic relations, a probation officer, a parole agent, a human resource developer, and a prison administrator. During his career, Ralph raised three children and coached a successful high school wrestling team. After retirement, Ralph completed a Master of Science and a Doctorate in Psychology.

Table of Contents

Introduction 7

Phenomenological Awareness 11

Verbal Representation................................... 18

Self-Regulation 24

The Structure of Personality 30

Cause and Effect in Personality 34

Balance in Personality............................... 37

Personality and Performance......................... 42

The Hermeneutic Spiral............................. 45

The Smorgasbord 50

Plug and Play 59

The Foundation of Personality 68

Appendix A 72

Introduction

Introduction

In his speech entitled *"Existentialism is a Humanism,"* Sartre describes man as someone who "...first exists: he materializes in the world, encounters himself, and only afterward defines himself... He will not be anything until later, then he will be what he makes of himself... Man is nothing other than his own project. He exists only to the extent he realizes himself, therefore he is nothing more than the sum of his actions... Responsible for what he is free condemned to be free... committing himself to life."

It is man, himself, that is charged with the development of his personality. Who we define ourselves to be determines what our life becomes.

I do not necessarily buy into the same understanding of Sartre's words that he may have intended. Sartre was an atheist who, in saying that *"existence precedes essence,"* takes any form of God out of the equation and acts as though there is no essence to existence until after personality forms. I disagree with this idea, but that is not a discussion for this writing because it doesn't matter where the continuum of development begins, only how it progresses. Of particular importance in this writing, to me, is how a personality evolves once a person takes charge of the evolution. Sartre points to the essence of life for a human as the intentional evolution of personality and he clearly indicates that he believes this to be the purpose of life. First, the realization that we can shape our own personality, then the challenge to find the path to actualization as we see it.

Dr. Carl Jung uses the term "Human Wholeness" to describe the integration of the conscious mind with the part of mind that is below consciousness. He believed that, until the material below consciousness is brought into consciousness and processed, a human could not experience wholeness, or balance. This process is important if you are to take control of your "self," but what are the tools that you need to grow yourself?

I turn to Edmund Husserl for the most critical tool that enables us to have a phenomenological experience of the "things" in our environment. Husserl described this phenomenological experience as a description of the essence of things that we experience. Bracketing is the first of three procedures that Husserl felt were necessary to appreciate a thing as it is. When we bracket, we set aside all preconceived ideas that could influence our perception and experience the thing as it is. The second procedure is called transcendental reduction and is the process of preparing a detailed description of a phenomenon's meaning and essence. The third procedure is called "free imaginative variation" and is the process of isolating the essential features of a thing and determining whether the thing would be the same if we removed the feature. I use this material as the foundation for a phenomenological rebirth of personality.

We *can* shape our own personality. We do it all the time. So, how does it work? Carl Jung called the process of individuation "Active Imagination." If you were to define the personality that would be necessary to actualize your life, what would it look like? Where would you begin? Would you pick qualities out of thin air, or would you build it like a house, from the ground up? Would you have a core of important qualities like resilience, self-efficacy, emotional intelligence, and critical thinking? Would you select values and principles that contribute to the greatest success? How would you make these qualities your own?

In the pages that follow, I hope to present you with a ground up approach to the development of personality through active imagination combined with a glossary of characteristics that can be picked out of thin air. If the foundation of personality is properly developed, followed by a thought process that carefully screens information and processes it for good decisions, and bolstered by an understanding of why we are here in the first place, then that personality will be able to adapt and adjust to the demands of life and control its own direction. If this sounds interesting, by all means, read on!

Phenomenological Awareness

Edmund Husserl describes phenomenology as the study of things "as they are." By "as they are," I believe that he meant to sense completely the entire reality of a thing and, in the case of thoughts, to sense the truth in the structure and meaning of the thought. The most unfiltered experience of our environment is found through the senses of sight, smell, hearing, taste, and touch. A sixth sense, intuition, is also part of this process. The senses have the innate ability to appreciate the environment without the cumbersome difficulty of language because they are designed to capture their data through awareness, not through definition.

Merriam-Webster describes the sense of sight as the physical sense by which light stimuli received by the eye are interpreted by the brain and constructed into a representation of the position, shape, brightness, and usually color of objects in space. The idea of physically seeing refers to the recognition of objects and things, but not to the definition of them. If we can just witness our environment without the difficulty of translating that experience into language, we could have an objective perception of the way a thing looks. The difficulty with sight is that things look different when viewed from a unique perspective. Take a table, for instance. When we sit at a table and look at it from the side, we see a trapezoid. If we look down from the top, we see a rectangle. From different angles around the table, we see different trapezoid shapes. The same is true of a tree, a rock, an animal, or any other form of existence that we might come across. In order to "see" an object, we must examine it from every angle to see it completely.

Hearing is the sense by which sounds are perceived, or the capacity to perceive sound. Sound waves are converted into nerve impulses through the ear for interpretation by the brain. The range of human hearing goes from 20 to 20,000 Hz, roughly. The **hertz** (symbol: **Hz**) is the unit of frequency in the International System of Units (SI) and is defined as one cycle per second. The hertz is an SI derived unit whose expression in terms of SI base units is s^{-1}, meaning that one hertz is the reciprocal of one second. When our ears are fully functioning, we pick up all of the sounds within our frequency range and can associate the sound with events and things in our environment.

Smell is the sense that enables one to perceive odors; it depends on the stimulation of sense organs in the nose by small particles carried in inhaled air. The ability to detect odor gives us a sense of how odor helps to clarify what a thing is. Nothing is just an odor, odor is associated with a thing, a process, and/or a place. The identification of specific odors with specific things, processes, and/or places, helps to clarify the relationships between things in our environment.

Taste is the perception produced or stimulated when a substance in the mouth reacts chemically with taste receptor cells located on taste buds in the oral cavity, mostly on the tongue. The ability to distinguish the taste of things allows us to identify the properties of things that we eat and drink, as well as those things that we ought not to eat.

Touch is the faculty by which external objects or forces are perceived through contact with the body (especially the hands). Although we most often associate touch with the hands, our entire body is a receptor for contact with our environment. Touch and sight enable us to locate objects in the space around us.

There is an old saying, from the doctrine of holism, that "the whole is greater than the sum of its parts." I believe that intuition is the 'whole" that is greater than the sum of the other senses. It is the awareness that gives us the ability to understand something immediately, without the need for conscious reasoning. Intuition takes the sum of the experience through our senses and adds a dimension that is greater than the sum of those senses. Although difficult to describe, intuition is a sense that is innate and functions as though our existence were an antenna that sends and receives signals through vibrations and experience. We sense the vibrations and react through our experience. The most difficult quality of intuition to understand is that we can know something that we have no earthly justification for knowing. It is just there. Psychologists and philosophers have struggled with this since the beginning of time. It is an animal-like instinct that defies definition, a soulful connection. Some people cultivate it like an essential element in the human condition. Most people avoid it like the plague because they can't see it or touch it. It is a link between the physical world and the spiritual world that can make us seem out of touch, if we give in to it too often, but it is a sense that can be cultivated in a healthy way. Ancient Egyptians had a saying, "all is in the All and the All is in all." Everything, and everyone, is connected and permeated by an energy field. We cannot separate from this. It is the intuitive sense that transcends our physical existence and leads us to a more complete understanding of our existence.

Each of these senses provides different information for the process of identifying and interacting with our environment. I mentioned sight and touch as senses that enable us to locate objects in space around us, but think of the combination of taste and smell. Take one of them away and what is the quality of your experience of food? When combined, each of the senses provides information that gives us a greater understanding of the things in our environment. If we are careful, we can get a complete experience of a thing by using all of our senses and allowing the thing to be what it is in the context of our senses. Events are a little more difficult because the experience of time makes the event more one-dimensional, but, if we are aware of this, we can attempt to gain a more comprehensive experience by moving with time to gather information from different angles and locations. Without the struggle to describe these phenomena with language, however, they are simply a personal experience.

The phenomenological appreciation of our environment must be translated into language in order for us to be able to share our experiences among us. To the extent that we do not fully appreciate our environment phenomenologically, we will fail to translate it properly into language and some of the truth will be lost simply because we didn't pay attention with all of our sensitive ability. To the extent that our ability to translate is limited by a limited vocabulary, or an inability to accurately depict our phenomenological experience in language, again, something is lost in translation.

To the extent that we are able to accurately experience our environment, and accurately translate that experience into verbal representation, we have an opportunity to act appropriately in response to that environment and the events that it presents. The challenge of this process is to produce the truth. The truth, for the purposes of this discussion, is the essence of what *is*. The truth is important because the closer to the truth we get, the more accurate and effective our behavior will be in response to the demands of our environment. This, in turn, will generate comfort as we negotiate our way through the demands of life. The further away from the truth that we get, the more out of touch we are with the reality that we are trying to manage and the more discomfort we experience.

In his book entitled "Phenomenology," Chad Engelland says, "truth happens." He goes on to say that "Truth happens in virtue of a fundamental openness marking the human being, an openness that offers a place for the things of the world to become manifest as the things that they are." In the physical world, or objective reality, truth lies in experiencing a thing as it is. This means applying all the senses to get the full experience of the thing. In the subjective world of personality, truth means belief. The accuracy of your beliefs, relative to the personality that you employ, depends on the clarity of your self-image. A self-image that is not carefully designed around beliefs that produce the behavior and end result that you are trying to manifest will fail to the extent that it is not clearly conceived and properly articulated.

The phenomenology of personality is a little more challenging than truth in our objective environment. In personality, seeing, hearing, feeling, tasting, and smelling, along with intuition, are symbolic, but the end result, or the truth in the thought, is just as critical to your reality as in physical phenomenology. I will go into further detail about this in later chapters, but the essence of this idea is that you "see," "taste," "hear," "smell," "touch," and "Intuit" with your mind.

Verbal Representation

Words are our verbal representation of the things in our world. As S. I. Hayakawa stated in his book, "Language in Thought and Action," the word is not the thing, it is a symbolic representation of the thing. If we learn to use language in a way that does not carefully describe the thing, the experience of the thing is lost in the wording. It is our responsibility to learn to use language in a way that properly describes the things we discuss.

Translating our experiences and our thoughts into verbal representation is very tricky and difficult because language is ambiguous and clumsy. If we use our example of a table, for instance, we tend to use the word "table." Yet the object that we are describing has so much more character than the word "table" can elicit in our mind. To properly describe the table, we would need to provide dimensions, materials used to construct the table, color, shape, intended use, and so on... We use the word "table" for brevity and because the characteristics of the table do not seem important in the overall message that we intend.

The unfortunate reality is that this process of using language, with brevity included in the usage, becomes a habit in every aspect of verbal representation and the full message is lost in the brevity. As a result, a great deal of what we call communication is based on assumption. The assumption that we understand what a person means by the use of the word "table," or the word mountain, or vehicle, or house, removes the actual shared experience of the thing from the realm of possibility. Each of these words are vague, without descriptors that illuminate the richness of their reality. True understanding cannot come from the careless use of language. It may be that understanding, true understanding, cannot come from language alone, at all. It may be that true understanding requires a phenomenological experience that accompanies the language. For instance, the use of the word table when you are in the same room as the table is much more effective than the use of the word when you are not. A complete description of the table requires a 360-degree, three-dimensional explanation. Even this does not guarantee an understanding of the table because the way an individual processes their experience often has bias and prejudice, built into the appreciation and translation of their environment and stored as an automatic habit, which creates blind spots that prevent a full appreciation. Communication can be very sticky.

Although my discussion of the translation of our experience into a verbal representation of it may sound a bit daunting, I mention the difficulties because it will be important to eliminate them, to the extent that this is possible, as we continue this discussion. This book is about the successful evolution of personality. We will not be successful at defining who we are if we take language for granted. Just like a phenomenological experience of our environment, we will need to be aware and accurate in our depiction of who we are, through a phenomenological appreciation of our description, if we are to evolve in a specific direction. Hold that thought.

Albert Bandura developed his Social Learning Theory around the concept of triadic reciprocal determinism. Triadic reciprocal determinism identifies three elements that interact in a reciprocal manner to develop personality. The three elements are the environment, the individual's perception of the environment, and the individual's interaction with the environment. Reciprocity lies in the bi-directional interaction between the environment, the individual, and the internalized perception of the interaction. The environment acts on the individual and the individual acts on the environment. This process is deterministic because, once the individual internalizes their experience with the environment, they can only act in accordance with the truth as they perceive it to be as a result of their experience of it. The mind cannot hold two opposing beliefs at the same time. So, the environment presents a scenario, the individual perceives the scenario, assesses it with the information currently stored in the subconscious mind, interacts with the scenario, tweaks their perception to support their currently dominant perception of the truth as a result of the interaction, and continues on. The individual cannot do anything other than make decisions that result from their currently held beliefs about the world, and themselves.

This process locks the individual in a behavior pattern that they are not even aware of because the psychological habits are in their subconscious. Now, let's switch back up to the "hold that thought" comment. You cannot have a phenomenological moment when you are filtering your experience through a lens in your subconscious mind. The lens is your currently dominant perception of the truth. Your currently dominant perception of the truth is made up of the collection of perceptions that you translated into language for the sake of brevity and that are now driving your awareness from your subconscious. Your experience is influenced by your current beliefs. Whew!

The point, in summary, is that we experience our environment (people, things, beliefs, etc.), assign verbal representation to the experience, stuff that verbal representation into our subconscious mind, and then act as though that verbal representation is the truth. We learn to assign verbal representation according to the degree of value that the people in our world, as we grow up, have for proper use of language and in terms of what *they* believe. It is their use of language, and their beliefs, that define how we use language, up until we realize how we have been programed.

Once we realize how we have been programmed, we can examine our use of language and relearn how to verbally represent our environment and our experience of it. We can then take control of the beliefs that we hold, learn how to evolve them according to the phenomenological experiences that we enjoy as we progress through our lives, and act in a new reality that serves the world as we perceive it to be. New subconscious habits and beliefs will develop as a result of this process. Our subconscious habits only belong to the environment that shaped us until that moment when we realize that we have the power to change through the choice of verbal representation that is more accurate for the life that we desire. The challenge, in my mind, is to experience our world phenomenologically in every possible instance. Clearly, the opportunity to experience phenomenologically is limited by the pace of our lives and it is necessary to have subconscious habits, but, wherever possible, the use of prejudgment and personal bias must be eliminated so that the experience can be appreciated for what it is.

It is critical to understand that the accurate depiction of our environment is important because it allows us to interact with that environment in an appropriate way. As I mentioned earlier, this reduces the amount of stress created by the demands the environment makes on us. It is equally critical that we accurately define who we are so that the person that is interacting with that environment is defined in a way that facilitates the management of that environment to produce the outcomes that we want in our lives. Who we are determines what we do.

Self-Regulation

Self-regulation is defined as "...the control of ones' own behavior through the use of self-monitoring (keeping a record of behavior), self-evaluation (assessing the information obtained during self-monitoring), and self-reinforcement (rewarding oneself for appropriate behavior or for attaining a goal." (APA College Dictionary of Psychology, p. 374, 2009) Personality is the mechanism that we use for self-regulation. Personality is defined as the "...enduring configuration of characteristics and behavior that comprises an individual's unique adjustment to life, including major traits, interests, drives, values, self-concept, abilities, and emotional patterns." (APA Dictionary of Psychology, 2019) Our personality is the sum of all of our experience and our perception of it. Every part of our personality has an effect on how we act in response to the demands and/or desires that exist in our relationship with our environment. Every decision that we make is the result of the understanding that we have of the world that we live in. As I said earlier, if that understanding, and to the extent that that understanding, is distorted, we are struggling with our interaction with the reality that we see and our comfort within it.

Words are the mechanism that we use to translate our experience into a medium of exchange that allows us to share that experience with other people. Words are also the medium of exchange that we use to talk to ourselves and about ourselves. The way we define our "selves" is the key to our performance. If you want to understand what I mean by this, listen for your "I am" statements. You tell people who you are all the time with those statements, but seldom listen to them as you say them. If you want to know your limitations, listen to how you define yourself.

I mentioned Bandura's triadic reciprocal determinism earlier. As we go through life, we pick up bits and pieces of language to represent our perception of the phenomenological experience of our environment. We assign some level of emotion to each experience, and to the words we use to describe those experiences. The verbal representations are seldom complete and the emotion that we assign is typically someone else's emotional value. So, we stumble through life with clipped verbal representations of the phenomena of experience, we have someone else's emotional intelligence, we are limited by our beliefs (that someone else put there), and we act in accordance with those beliefs as though they were true. People with a value for freedom will have a field day with this. How can you be free when you don't even own your own beliefs?

Self-regulation is the process of negotiating/managing your way through your environment through the control of your thoughts, behavior, and emotions. The closer you are to seeing the truth, the smoother you navigate. The more openly you can experience your environment, and the more precisely you can describe it, the better your chances of finding the truth. Properly identifying the truth around you, assigning the proper emotion to your situation, and interacting effectively with your environment is the result of proper self-regulation.

The truth about you is an important part of self-regulation. The interesting thing about you is that you are malleable, the truth in the environment is more objective. By malleable, I mean that you are who you are because you believe what you believe. I am not talking about how tall you are, or how much you weigh, those are the environmental qualities of your existence. I am talking about your personality, what you believe about yourself. Your self-talk creates your self-image, and your self-image creates performance (Lou Tice, 1983). The way you define yourself determines the way you interact with your environment and how smoothly you roll.

Let's take a simple example. If your partner does something that you don't like, you have any number of choices that you can make in response. Suppose you choose anger because that is what you have always chosen in similar situations, perhaps that is what your parents chose. The result of your anger is that you say something hurtful and mean. Your partner loses some respect and admiration for you as a result. You chose anger because it was a subconscious habit that defined who you are. If you lose a precious relationship because you relied on a habit that is toxic, where does that leave you? I feel like I have to share a lesson I learned as a young soldier in Vietnam. Our team was on the range, one day, and I was missing my target with an M-60 machine gun, which is hard to do. I began to cuss, and an old soldier came over to me and he said, "Anger is always preceded and followed by stupidity. You get stupid on a mission and endanger the lives of our team members and I will shoot you myself!" Needless to say, I never forgot that lesson.

So, how many possible alternatives are there to anger? Here is the key to self-regulation. There are as many alternatives as you have time to consider. If you can hold your emotions at bay, you have plenty of time to choose a different alternative. Emotional intelligence is the ability to assign an appropriate amount of emotion to the situation that presents. The appropriate amount of emotion is connected to the desired outcome as well as the situation. I don't want to get too deeply into emotional intelligence here, but it is important to note that emotional intelligence can easily override actual intelligence and cause a loss of control of the situation.

Regulation is a revolving dance with the environment, as described by Bandura's triadic reciprocal determinism. Every second of your existence is immersed in this dance. The skills that you use to define you are the tools of your regulation. When you realize that you can add any tools that you want, you can prepare yourself for any set of circumstances. If you truly want to be free, having all the necessary tools for the job of life determines how much freedom you can actually achieve. Of course, you have to have a concept of what freedom really is, too.

The ability to regulate your way through life's challenges, to manifest the life that you want for yourself and your family, can be developed with a roadmap that points the way. The real challenge, though, is whether a person is willing to take the responsibility for who they are and for the work it takes to remake themselves into more of who they can be. We talk a lot about being responsible and taking responsibility for our choices as adults, but do we believe that we can change and are we willing to take responsibility for that change. This can be a little scary.

The Structure of Personality

Personality may seem like a helter-skelter kind of a mess, when first examined, but, in reality, it is a mechanism that works through the same kind of behavior that the senses use to communicate with the environment. If you think in terms of the sense of touch, when we touch something, a sensation moves from the point of contact, up through our nervous system, into the brain stem, and then into the brain. Personality works in much the same way. We perceive something, the perception runs to our subconscious mind for comparisons, we make an identification, then rummage through our mind for similarities and past methods of interaction, and we choose a behavior that we think manages the perception. This mind behavior is parallel to the physical behavior that results from touch.

I use an analogy of a tree to symbolize the structure of personality that I think is most representative of how it works. If we think of the roots of the tree as the foundation of personality, the trunk of the tree as the core mechanical devices of personality, the branches as the various interests of the personality, and the leaves as the changing information relative to those interests, we can see how personality might resemble a tree. We can go further into this analogy by drawing a comparison to community and the things that surround the tree and even discussing the various types of trees to separate personalities into types, but, for my purposes here, the tree, itself, is my focus.

The roots of the tree symbolize the values and principles that we are taught by family and community. The idea of value can be extended to things and/or ideas. We may value nice clothes, a home, an automobile, and we may also value freedom, honesty, integrity, and many other things. We may learn to live by the principles of truth, integrity, honesty, or manipulation, deceit, and distortion. Whatever we learn to value becomes a part of our foundational fabric. Our principles become the rules we live by and determine whether we obtain the things we value. Success or failure results from the consistency, or inconsistency, between values and principles. The qualities that we build in here determine what kind of tree we are.

The trunk of the tree represents the core of our personality. Here we find the self-regulating things that give us strength to face the world in pursuit of the things we value. Critical thinking, or some version of it, lies here. Resilience, self-efficacy, and emotional intelligence lie here. These mechanisms help us to analyze, and select responses, to the events and demands that the environment presents to us. They also provide the characteristics that keep us stable while we bounce around in the environment, making mistakes, learning, re-engaging, and shaping our path as we go. If we have a good combination of characteristics here, we are better equipped to negotiate our way through our environment.

The branches of the tree represent all of the various interests and necessities that we develop as we journey through life. Each branch is a pathway to the information that we find in the leaves, or the storage areas in our brain that contain the information that we collect relative to our various interests and beliefs. Interestingly, the leaves fall off seasonally, much the same as the evolution of the information that we save relative to our various interests and necessities.

I could go on with this analogy, but I think you can see my point. There is a structure, often informal, but more powerful when it is formal, that drives us through this thing called life. When we understand that this thing is built by the environment, initially, and realize that it can be built intentionally by our own actions, we have evolved from a personality that is driven by our environment to a personality that drives itself.

Cause and Effect in Personality

Every cause has an effect, and every effect has a cause. Every effect becomes a cause. When we look at this evolutionary chain we see a continuum, or a ripple, that repeats from cause to effect, to cause then effect, and so on, throughout the life of a personality. If we think of this in terms of Bandura's triadic reciprocal determinism, we see an event in our environment, we have a perception of the event, we perform a behavior associated with the event, and then form a perception, as a result of the event, that either modifies an existing perception or defines an initial one. When the process repeats, it becomes a habit. Once these habits are formed, our future is determined by what they are. We can only make decisions that are supported by these habits. This cycle continues with the information lodged in our subconscious having an effect on our perception going forward and becoming, therefore, a cause.

When we recognize this process as one that is initially controlled by the environment, and one that controls our ability to function in that environment, the realization may cause us to wonder at how much more effective we might be if we took control of the person involved in the process. The idea that we might manage causation in our lives is exciting because it opens the door to unlimited growth potential and provides an opportunity to own the responsibility for our personal development. Left to the environment, we remain limited to only those things our immediate surroundings expose us to and the perception of that environment that has been made for us. If we take control of the process, we dictate how we perceive the environment.

The environment consists of everything and everyone that comes into contact with our lives. When we place ourselves in a location and mindset that limits growth, or develop a circle of friends and acquaintances who inhibit growth, we stifle our ability to develop to our full potential, or in that direction, since actualization is not possible under these circumstances. Taking control of those factors offers us the optimistic condition of arranging those things and people so that we may develop a reality for growth in the direction of actualization toward that which we envision. It may sound as though I am suggesting a sort of cruelty, but my purpose is to show the power of cause and effect and to introduce the reality that everything we think, do, accept, believe, or invite into our environment, shapes the life we live.

The impact of cause and effect is at work in all that we do. It either works quietly on its own, through our subconscious, or intentionally, under our conscious control in cooperation with our subconscious mind. The only way that we know how we are shaping our lives is by bringing this process out of the subconscious and reformatting it, consciously, so the subconscious habits are changed to move us toward the life that we choose. Remembering that we are creating chains of cause and effect, we must constantly cultivate the habits and perceptions that move us toward the cause and effect that drive us toward the growth that produces the life that we want.

Balance in Personality

When we think about balance, as in standing on one foot, it is the ability to maintain an equal distribution of weight. Balance, relative to human existence, is about having the elements of physical, mental, and spiritual qualities in balance. Each of these elements has its own balance to maintain and then is influenced by balance, or lack of balance, with the others.

Physiological balance is the balance of the parts of the body. There is a muscular, a skeletal, an organ, and a nervous system, each that requires its own balance and, in turn, balances with the others. It doesn't really serve the purpose of this book to get too involved in the nature of physiological balance, but suffice it to say that there is such a balance and that being out of balance reduces the organisms' capabilities to the extent of the lack of balance. For example, each motion of the body has a corresponding opposite motion. When the strength of one side of the motion is disproportionately stronger, or weaker, than the other side, muscles are torn, or movement is distorted. When organs are not secreting properly, the imbalance in hormones causes any number of illnesses from diabetes to kidney disease, cystic fibrosis, cancer, etc.

Neurological problems result in misfiring muscles, neuropathy, epilepsy, learning disabilities, autism, brain tumors, etc. Skeletal problems result in osteoporosis and osteoarthritis, etc. It is clear that there is a need for balance and health in each of these physical systems.

Mental balance is the focus of this book. I define mental balance as a balance between the phenomenological appreciation of the environment, the verbal representation of that appreciation, the perceptions that develop as a result of the verbal representations, the evolution of those representations, and the resulting perceptions and behaviors. Balance occurs when the verbal representations closely resemble the truth of the phenomenological experience and the perceptions that develop accurately represent the environment so that the responses to the environment are accurate, as well.

Spiritual balance is more difficult to define. I would like to go back, before the construction of religions, to a time when Egypt was the seat of knowledge. Hermes Trismegistus was credited with having said that the "all is in the All, and the All is in all." By this, Hermes meant that everything exists in the mind of the All (God) and the All (God) is in everything. I like this idea because it basically says that there is a great body of energy that we are suspended in and that our energy is derived from that source to drive our bodies. If we think of that energy as the mind of God, then our energy is a piece of the mind of God, a soul. We cannot be separated from God, and He cannot be separated from us. Balance, then, when talking about the soul, means some affinity for a higher power, a recognition that there is something beyond our existence that we can be in harmony with.

Beyond the need to balance each of these individually is a need to balance all of them together. The mind drives the body while the spirit drives the mind. A well-maintained body, integrated with a mind that is accurate in perception, translation, and communication, permeated by a spirit that is regularly polished and kept clean, the human condition can be high functioning for an extended period of time. Maintaining balance is a critical function in the quality and duration of the life experience.

Balance, relative to personality, means that the foundation, the skill set, and the quality of information that combine to regulate existence are in harmony both internally and with the external world. In order for this to occur, each of these elements must be carefully constructed.

The foundation of personality, as mentioned above, lies in the values, principles, and self-regulating mechanisms that an individual learns through their environment. Values are the things we think are important. They include the way we treat other people, the things we like, the things we stand for, etc. Principles are the rules we live by. Manners, respect for others, right vs wrong, ethical behavior, honor, integrity, all are part of a person's principles. Self-regulating mechanisms are mechanisms that regulate how we interact with our environment. Resilience, emotional intelligence, self-efficacy, motivation, and willpower are all self-regulating mechanisms. It is said that the entire personality is a self-regulating mechanism.

When I speak of "skill set," I mean the way a person thinks. Critical thinking is a term that we often associate with clean thinking. Learning how to identify a need for a decision, generating knowledge about the issues involved in the decision, crystalizing the issues, generating alternative solutions and the accompanying anticipated outcomes, and choosing the solution that offers the outcome you seek, are all parts of the process of thinking. Formal and informal logic are also a part of thinking. Formal logic follows the rules of logic while informal logic tends to rely on "common sense." The best-case scenario would apply formal logic to the process of critical thinking. The bottom line is that the cleaner your thinking process, the clearer the identification of the problem, the more effective the generation of alternative solutions, the clearer the anticipation of outcomes, and the clearer the selection of the solution, the more effective is the navigation through life.

Personality and Performance

The relationship between personality and performance is a cause-and-effect relationship. Personality is the cause and performance is the effect. Performance is any behavior or process that is carried out to accomplish an action, a task, or complete a function. Performance can be physical, mental, or spiritual. I shared the definition of personality earlier. It is the "...enduring configuration of characteristics and behavior that comprises an individual's unique adjustment to life, including major traits, interests, drives, values, self-concept, abilities, and emotional patterns." (APA Dictionary of Psychology, 2019) Personality determines performance. Who we believe we are determines what we are able to do. This is a little tricky to understand because the application is an abstract application. The characteristics of personality that make performance possible are things like critical thinking, intrinsic motivation, resilience, emotional intelligence, will-power, determination, dedication, perseverance, etc., that all combine to make up self-image.

I am going to borrow a few lines from a program developed by Lou Tice (1983), called *Investment in Excellence.* "The mind doesn't know the difference between the truth and what you tell it. We act in accordance with the truth as we believe it to be, not necessarily the truth. Self-talk creates self-image, self-image creates performance, performance creates self-talk." (Tice, 1983) These statements were made about personality. We are who we are because we believe that this is who we are. Belief can be changed because it is not an objective truth. It is subjective.

If who we are produces a particular level of performance and we want to change that performance, we must change our beliefs about ourselves. Once we understand that the things we believe about ourselves are only true because we believe them to be true, we can see our way to making the changes in our beliefs that will cause a change in our performance.

An example of this might be something like I want to start a consulting business, but I am afraid to plunge into this unfamiliar territory because I am not comfortable with the possibility of failure. If I am going to be successful, I must overcome this fear by doing several things. First, I should research those areas of consulting that I am not familiar with; accounting, public speaking, networking, promoting my work, marketing, etc. Then I have to see myself as that person who enjoys the challenge of learning and creating in the area of my expertise. My self-talk will need to sound like, "I enjoy speaking to groups about my product." "I love the challenge of breaking new barriers." "I learn new topics easily." "I get help with areas that I am unfamiliar with."

You can see that the way I define myself has to contribute to the successful achievement of my vision. My vision is the end result, or where I want to be. For instance, if I were to describe the house I want to live in simply as a three bedroom, two bath house with a two-car garage, it would be difficult to find the house because there are so many houses that fit those criteria. If I describe the house as a one story, three-bedroom house, with two baths, a two-car garage, with two bedrooms on one end of the house and a master bedroom on the other, that has a kitchen in the center of the house with a wrap-around marble counter, KitchenAid appliances and is painted white, you see how it narrows down the number of houses that fit the criteria. In the same way we crystalize a vision of the house we want, we must have a vision of the person that we will need to be to achieve whatever it is we want to achieve. As with the house, the vision of the person we need to be must be so clear that we can become that person easily.

The Hermeneutic Spiral

Hermeneutics is the study of the meaning of words to interpret text and understand what meaning was intended by the author. The essence of hermeneutics has been described using the doctrine of holism: we can only understand the parts of a text, or any body of meaning, out of a general idea of its whole, yet we can only gain this understanding of the whole by understanding its parts. Gadamer proposed that the fundamental issue of understanding and interpretation lies in the study of conditions for understanding and interpretation through understanding experience in general.

In order for there to be a hermeneutic interpretation, there would have to have been a hermeneutic formulation. Hermeneutics, and holism, in psychology, is the study of how the individual experiences their world and learns to verbally represent that world. Personality is the result of evolving hermeneutic circles. Personality is the "whole" while all of the events that help to shape that personality, and the perception of the meaning of those events, are the parts.

All of human life is reflected in the hermeneutic spiral that creates meaning for that life. If we examine the work of Bandura (1971), as mentioned earlier, we see that his triadic reciprocal determinism is a hermeneutic circle. In Bandura's circle we have the environment, our perception of the environment witnessed phenomenologically and represented verbally, and our interaction with the environment. According to Bandura, these three elements revolve in a loop that evolves our personality.

Another hermeneutic circle is described in the work of Lou Tice (1983). In the case of Tice's circle, self-talk creates self-image, self-image creates performance, and performance creates self-talk. These three elements also evolve to develop personality, according to Tice.

I would like to propose a hermeneutic "spiral," as opposed to a circle, that begins with the phenomenological experience of the environment. Each individual has a phenomenological experience of the environment that is, initially, only sensory. Science tells us that the fetus begins to react to stimuli in the womb long before birth. These experiences affect the development of the fetus and the eventual development of personality. If the host parent suffers trauma, the fetus suffers with the experience of anxiety and the physical manifestation of that anxiety, i.e., adrenaline, neural excitement, other hormones, etc. The fetus does not have the ability to verbally represent their experience, so the experience is etched in their subconscious without an explanation and becomes a cause for behavioral effects well into the life of the child.

Through the first few years, the infant/toddler responds to their environment without the use of language, or phenomenologically, and they record feelings that they associate with events, much the same as the fetus. As the child ages, language is introduced to represent the experience. Each experience is filtered through our existing self-image, which includes those phenomenological experiences from the pre-language era and the developing verbal representations, then we interact with the environment, we develop self-talk resulting from that interaction with the environment, our self-image begins to develop, we experience the beginning of self-esteem, and then we begin another loop. Keeping in mind that there are many of these loops occurring simultaneously, we can see how our personality can become fragmented by all of the stimuli that confront us in a constant demand for our attention. In reality, there is a great deal of fragmentation built into the process of becoming a personality. The key is to stay grounded in our roots and core self-regulating mechanisms as we experience each of these loops. Along with self-talk, we accumulate information about the world that shapes our perception of it, and we develop opinions. Opinions and bias are built into our appreciation of our environment, and we have a phenomenological appreciation that is distorted by our opinions and biases.

I describe these hermeneutic phenomena as a spiral, as opposed to a circle, because a circle is two dimensional while the process of personal evolution is spread out over time and is three dimensional. In our early years, as we begin to learn how to represent our environment verbally, the spiral is very tight, and learning takes place very quickly. As we approach our mid-years, learning slows down and the spiral is more open. In our later years, the spiral opens up even more as learning continues to slow down.

Once a personality has been shaped by experience, beliefs, opinions, and subconscious habits, change can become very difficult. Tice believed that it would take a significant emotional experience to cause a person to change. I believe that the desire to change can be the result of an intellectual understanding of personality, and how it affects performance, and can be just as powerful as a significant emotional experience. The process may be difficult, at first, but, once we become familiar with it, and change our beliefs, and our intention, change itself can become a subconscious habit.

The Smorgasbord

Often our first thought, when we think of a smorgasbord, is food. I use the term, here, to represent all of the possible characteristics that can be integrated into a personality. A characteristic is a feature or quality of a person. Characteristics combine to form a personality. At the point where we become aware that we can control the characteristics in our personality, we have the ability to pick and choose what those characteristics are. In this chapter I present a list of possible characteristics, and their definitions, to offer some options and give an example of what kinds of things are characteristics. This list is not exhaustive. There are many other characteristics that are available. Pick up your lexicon and read through it. You will be amazed at the possibilities. It is my hope that each reader will see what a characteristic is and will feel empowered to search for the qualities that will make them the best person that they can be.

o **Abstinence:** The act of refraining from the use of something, particularly alcohol or drugs, or from participation in sexual or other activity.

o **Accommodation:** Adjustment or modification.

- **Achievement Motivation:** The desire to perform well and be successful.

- **Active Listening:** Listening closely and attentively, and asking questions, to fully understand the content and message in conversation.

- **Adaptation:** Modification to suit different or changing circumstances.

- **Altruism:** An apparently unselfish concern for others or behavior that provides benefit to others at some cost to the individual.

- **Ambivalence:** The simultaneous existence of contradictory feelings and attitudes, such as friendliness and hostility, toward the same person, object, event, or situation.

- **Anger:** An emotion characterized by tension and hostility arising from frustration, real or imagined injury by another, or perceived injustice.

- **Brainstorming:** A problem-solving strategy in which ideas are generated spontaneously and uninhibitedly, usually in a group setting, without any immediate critical judgement about their potential value.

o **Code of Ethics:** A set of Standards and principles of conduct.

o **Creative Intelligence:** The set of skills used to create, invent, discover, explore, imagine and suppose.

o **Critical Thinking:** A form of directed, problem-focused thinking in which the individual tests ideas or possible solutions for errors or drawbacks.

o **Data Collection:** A systematic gathering of information for research or practical purposes.

o **Deception:** Any distortion of fact with the purpose of misleading others.

o **Decision Making:** The cognitive process of choosing between two or more alternatives.

o **Determination:** Firm or fixed intention to achieve a desired end result.

o **Discipline:** Training that corrects, molds, or perfects the mental faculties or moral character.

o **Eclecticism:** A theoretical or practical approach

that blends, or attempts to blend, diverse conceptual formulations or techniques into an integrated approach.

o **Ego Strength:** The ability of the EGO to maintain an effective balance between the inner impulses of the ID, the SUPEREGO, and outer reality. An individual with a strong ego is thus one who is able to tolerate frustration and stress, postpone gratification, modify selfish desires when necessary, and resolve internal conflicts and emotional problems before they lead to neurosis.

o **Emotional intelligence:** The ability to process emotional information and use it in reasoning and other cognitive functions. It comprises four abilities: to perceive and appraise emotions accurately; to access and evoke emotions when they facilitate cognition; to comprehend emotional language and make use of emotional information; and to regulate one's own emotions to promote growth and well-being.

o **Energetic:** Operating with or marked by vigor.

o **Facilitator:** A professional or lay member of a group who fulfills some or all of the functions of a group leader.

- **Fitness:** A set of attributes that people have or are able to achieve relating to their ability to perform physical work and to carry out daily tasks with vigor and alertness, without undo fatigue, and with ample energy to enjoy leisure pursuits.

- **Flow:** A state of optimal experience arising from intense involvement in an activity that is enjoyable, such as playing a sport, performing a musical passage, or writing a creative piece. Flow arises when one's skills are fully utilized yet equal to the demands of the task, intrinsic motivation is at a peak, one loses self-consciousness and temporal awareness, and one has a sense of total control, effortlessness, and complete concentration.

- **Generalization:** The process of deriving a concept, judgment, principle, or theory from a limited number of specific cases and applying it more widely, often to an entire class of objects, events, or people.

- **Happiness:** An emotion of joy, gladness, satisfaction, and well-being.

- **Identity:** An individual's sense of self defined by (a) a set of physical and psychological characteristics that is not wholly shared with any other person and (b) a range of social and interpersonal affiliations (e.g., ethnicity) and social roles.

o **Ideology:** A systematic ordering of ideas with associated doctrines, attitudes, beliefs, and symbols that together form a more or less coherent philosophy for a person, group, or sociopolitical movement.

o **Independence:** Not subject to control by others.

o **Intense:** Existing in an extreme degree.

o **Kindness:** Benevolent and helpful action intentionally directed toward another person.

o **Learning:** The process of acquiring new and relatively enduring information, behavior patterns, or abilities, characterized by modification of behavior as a result of practice, study, or experience.

o **Logic:** the branch of epistemology that is concerned with the forms of argument by which a valid conclusion may be drawn from accepted premises.

o **Methodology:** The science of method or orderly

arrangement; specifically, the branch of logic concerned with the application of the principles of reasoning to scientific inquiry. The system of methods, principles, and rules of procedure used within a particular discipline.

o **Mindfulness:** Full awareness of one's internal states and surroundings: the opposite of absent-mindedness.

o **Narcissism:** Excessive self-love or egocentrism.

o **Noble:** Possessing very high or excellent qualities or properties.

o **Objective:** Expressing or detailing with facts or conditions as perceived without distortion by personal feelings, prejudices, or interpretations.

o **Obstinate:** Perversely adhering to an opinion, purpose, or course in spite of reason, arguments, or persuasion.

o **Perseverance:** To persist in a state, enterprise, or undertaking in spite of counterinfluences, opposition, or discouragement.

o **Persistence:** Continuing without change in function or structure.

- **Phenomenological Awareness:** Search for the elusive essence of things and wonder concerning the possibility of experiencing things, as they are.

- **Resilient:** Tending to recover from misfortune or change.

- **Resourceful:** Capable of devising ways and means.

- **Responsible:** Moral, legal, or mental accountability; reliability and trustworthiness.

- **Self-efficacy:** An individual's belief in their capacity to act in ways necessary to reach specific goals.

- **Self-esteem:** Confidence and satisfaction in one's self.

- **Teachable:** Capable of being taught and willing to learn.

- **Technical:** A person who understands automation and can navigate and interact with AI.

- **Tenacious:** Persistent in maintaining, adhering to, or seeking something valued or desired.

- **Thorough:** Carried through to completion.

These potential characteristics are just a sample. Who do you need to be to achieve your vision for yourself?

Plug and Play

If you are to build a personality that delivers the life that you envision, then you must understand what qualities of personality are required in order to deliver that life and you must have a process that integrates those qualities into your current personality. This process must also provide a method for eliminating old psychological habits that prevent you from developing toward that enhanced personality.

If you were to go house shopping, without some idea of what the house you want would be like, you might search for a long time trying to find a house that feels right. If you know what the house you want should be like before you shop, you can limit your search to only those houses that meet your criteria. To accomplish this, you develop a floor plan, visualize each room, identify special materials for each room, visualize the outside of the house, with landscaping and decking, finish materials, driveway, garage, etc. The more crystalized your perception of what your house should look and feel like, the fewer houses that you will need to view.

The realization of personality is the same. If you have a good vision of who you need to be to achieve the life that you desire, then you can easily build the characteristics of that personality into your own personality and achieve the lifestyle that you want. Understanding the hermeneutic spiral, belief in your ability to create your own spiral, and determination to be the person who delivers the life you want, are the necessary foundational elements. Once you have these elements, you can accurately evolve a personality that will deliver the performance that you are looking for by building in the characteristics that produce the necessary performance. In the following pages, I will identify the steps in this process and show you how to manage the change that you feel you need to make.

Keep in mind that life is a trial-and-error experience. It either evolves according to environmental factors or it evolves according to your ability to accurately determine what characteristics you need and plug them in to your personality. The intentional evolution of personality depends on your understanding of what human characteristics produce what performance and, on your ability, to build those characteristics into your personality. You will make mistakes. The challenge is to keep evolving.

The process described in these pages depends on your belief in change and your desire to change. If you have those prerequisites, you can take control of your personality, through the process that I provide in the pages that follow, and become the person who performs in a way that produces the outcomes that you want. The process is simple and, once you own it and trust yourself, you will be able to make instantaneous changes. It will take a little practice, but the end result will be worth it.

This book began with a discussion of the phenomenological appreciation of our environment. The process of change in the environment begins with a phenomenological experience of the environment, then is transformed to a verbal representation of that experience, then there is an action, or interaction, with the environment with an associated emotion. The process begins with a new experience and then repeats the experience with the previous experience acting as a filter so that each succeeding experience adds to the earlier experiences but is also influenced by those experiences. The environment is full of rich interactions with things, people, places, activities, and interactions that combine in a potentially infinite number of evolving spirals.

Personality can be intentionally evolved using the same kind of sequence. When you examine your personality from a phenomenological perspective, however, your senses are applied in a different way than the way the senses are applied to our physical environment.

To "see" our selves means to examine the unique

characteristics that make us who we are. Sight, from this point of view, combines the verbal representation of self with the mental performance of self. We "see" who we are in our mind's eye through thoughts. We "hear" by listening to the way we define ourselves. This is often heard in "I am..." statements, but can also be an internal voice that reminds us of who we are. "Taste" is more of a value statement in the phenomenology of personality, but it defines the quality of our existence. If something tastes right in personality, it flows well and feels right. "Touch" is symbolic of our feelings associated with who we are and the emotion that drives our self-image. When we are in touch with our feelings and our self-image, we are aware. "Smell" is the most difficult sense to translate in the phenomenology of thought because, like taste, it has symbolic value. There is a synthesis of the senses of smell, taste, and touch into a sense of what is "right."

A simple example of this phenomenological appreciation to developing a skill might be found in the concept of resilience. If we see the word, feel the phenomena of resilience, gain a sense of what this concept means, how we apply it in our lives, and how it feels, we can tell our "selves" that we have acquired this skill. We can then repeat the experience of the concept in our mind until we are living a resilient life by applying the concept to everything we do. In the following paragraphs, I will attempt to take you through this process, step by step, to help you make it a habit in your life.

Resilience is "the process and outcome of successfully adapting to difficult or challenging life experiences, especially through mental, emotional, and behavioral flexibility and adjustment to external and internal demands." (APA College Dictionary of Psychology, 2009, p. 354) The common definition is simply bouncing back from adversity. If we are to own the concept of resilience in order to make it work through our subconscious mind, we must understand each of the concepts presented in the definition and then be able to "feel" resilient sensually. I will give an example from my life that makes resilience live for me.

I began the journey to be a Doctor of Psychology in 2018. Adapting to the demands of the doctoral process meant that I needed to recognize the external demands of the process and adjust my internal demands to meet the requirements of those external demands. The first two years were courses in my primary focus (performance psychology), statistics, research methods, and courses that taught how to choose a topic, develop a study, and manage the process. The mental, emotional, and behavioral flexibility necessary to navigate this journey can cripple some of the greatest minds because the rigor of the process is brutal.

I had a committee with a Chair, a content expert, and a statistical methods expert who reviewed every phase of the study and sent me back to the drawing board more times than I care to mention. There is a format for everything. My idea and design were scrutinized and hammered until the idea clearly represented something new in my area of research and the design was the right fit for the study. I would submit what I believed to be the appropriate description of my study and would get it back with comments that required that I retool the entire study. Then the study had to be approved by a gatekeeper for the University. Major changes were required, again. I was drained mentally, emotionally, physically, and spiritually for weeks at a time. I cannot lie, there were times when I wanted to quit. But quitting is not in my DNA and that was the key to my successful completion of the program.

Resilience is the ability to keep getting back up. I read a Samurai quote once that said: *"Knocked down seven times, get up eight."* We do this mentally when we find that our mental preparation caused us to fail. Recognizing that our current mindset does not have the correct combination of information to successfully complete a task is an opportunity to restructure our mental beliefs and acquire any necessary skills that we don't currently have in our toolbox.

Emotional intelligence is the process of investing the appropriate kind and amount of emotion for the circumstances that present. It is defined more succinctly in the APA College Dictionary of Psychology as: ...the ability to process emotional information and use it in reasoning and other cognitive processes. It comprises four abilities: to perceive and appraise emotions accurately; to access and evoke emotions when they facilitate cognition; to comprehend emotional language and make use of emotional information; and to regulate one's own and others' emotions to promote growth and well-being." (APA College Dictionary of Psychology, 2009).

I put all of this in here because it is part of understanding resilience. I was on an emotional rollercoaster for five years and I had to learn how to regulate those emotions so that the outcomes were positive and productive. I felt anger, frustration, elation, confidence, doubt, and more. I experienced a reformation of my personality that enabled me to become accepting and determined no matter what the circumstances. I stopped thinking about whether I was worthy by realizing that worthiness had nothing to do with the journey.

Behaviorally I was tossed back and forth in a turmoil of ideas that were, at times, contradictory and, at other times, synchronous. The challenge was to make myself into a person who is results oriented and who simply reports what is seen. I was being challenged to let the thing be itself and to see it as itself. I went through the frightening realization that I had carried a set of beliefs my entire life that were now being challenged because I was learning that bias and prejudgment were errors of thought. I had to realize that much of what I thought I knew was purely belief without concrete evidence. I had to change the way I thought, and what I thought, which changed the way I act.

Spiritually I was forced to reaffirm my faith that the universe is unfolding as it should. I had to stay in the process and feel the flow of it. Fortunately, my faith in the power of the Great One never wavered. I mention all of these things to help with the experience of resilience. It is not simply bouncing back from adversity; it is the integration of all of the things that contribute to the ability to bounce back. Feeling all of this is the essence of resilience. To say "I am resilient" means that I understand all of these factors and that I am these factors. If you are resilient, you have the skills to adapt to any set of circumstances and continue to move forward. Plug and Play!

The Foundation of Personality

There are a few things that every personality should never be without. Resilience, as discussed earlier, is one of those things. Another critical ingredient is critical thinking. Critical thinking is a form of directed, problem-focused thinking in which the individual tests ideas or possible solutions for errors or drawbacks (APA College Dictionary of Psychology, p. 91, 2009). A good thinker identifies and clarifies a problem, generates possible solutions, anticipates outcomes, and selects the alternative that offers the best possible solution. Having a process for making good decisions is a key to arriving at solutions that give you the best chance at success.

Another important ingredient is emotional intelligence. I mentioned this as a piece of resilience, but it is much more than that. It is its own reward. When you are in control of your emotions and can measure them out to meet the circumstances that you are faced with, you keep your emotions from overriding your reason intelligence. This is important because emotions can distort a situation and prevent the effective management of it. I mentioned earlier that, as a young soldier in Vietnam, I was told that anger is always preceded and followed by stupidity. Without going through the story again, an old soldier was trying to teach me that anger in combat caused irrational behavior that could get people killed. I am not saying that there aren't any situations where anger might be useful, I am saying that anger often signals that you have reached the end of your skill level. When we get angry, and allow our emotions to dictate our decisions, we often say and do things that we later regret. You can't take back words or deeds that are said and done in anger.

Self-efficacy is another critical element in personality. Self-efficacy is an individual's capacity to act effectively to bring about desired results (APA College Dictionary of Psychology, p. 372, 2009). As you can see, self-efficacy is closely tied to resilience and emotional intelligence. The combination of critical thinking, self-efficacy, resilience, and emotional intelligence provides a foundation for personality that enables us to search for the qualities that shape our lives. Although each of these characteristics of self-regulation incorporate many additional qualities, the successful generation of these mechanisms provides a stability that is necessary for the process of self-reformation. The process of change depends on the confidence to experiment and reality test with qualities that you think will take you where you want to go.

To this list I would add hermeneutic awareness, or an understanding of how words are used, how bias interferes with the phenomenological appreciation of things, and how to glean your own understanding of things through the understanding of language. Cognitive flexibility, positive anticipation, possibility thinking, and objectivity are also desirable.

Values and principles are an essential part of the foundation of personality. I mentioned them earlier in my tree analogy. I can't tell you what values and principles are important in your pursuit of your purpose, but I can say that they will determine your success. The lack of principle in the development of personality will result in failures on your chosen path. Values that are not in harmony with principles will also produce failure. Although life is a succession of trial and error, the error can be reduced through these elements.

Courage is the product of belief and faith. Belief in your ability to bounce back from adversity, in your ability to manage emotion, in your "self" as a catalyst, and in your ability to reason through the demands of everyday life are essential elements in the process of moving forward. Faith that everything will work out is the ingredient that provides hope and optimism when you can't see clearly what the next step must be. The tools in this book provide a practical guide to change but, without courage, nothing can be gained.

Steven Covey, in *The Seven Habits of Highly Effective*

People, invited us to: (1) Be Proactive; (2) Begin with the End in Mind; (3) Put First Things First; (4) Think Win-Win; (5) Seek First to Understand, Then to be Understood; (6) Synergize; and (7) Sharpen the Saw. If you combine these habits with a process that facilitates change, there is no limit to who you can become or what you can achieve.

Plug and play!

Appendix A

Desiderata: Original Text

This is the original text from the book where Desiderata was first published.

Go placidly amid the noise and the haste, and remember what peace there may be in silence. As far as possible, without surrender, be on good terms with all persons.

Speak your truth quietly and clearly; and listen to others, even to the dull and the ignorant; they too have their story.

Avoid loud and aggressive persons; they are vexatious to the spirit. If you compare yourself with others, you may become vain or bitter, for always there will be greater and lesser persons than yourself.

Enjoy your achievements as well as your plans. Keep interested in your own career, however humble; it is a real possession in the changing fortunes of time.

Exercise caution in your business affairs, for the world is full of trickery. But let this not blind you to what virtue there is; many persons strive for high ideals, and everywhere life is full of heroism.

Be yourself. Especially do not feign affection. Neither be cynical about love; for in the face of all aridity and disenchantment, it is as perennial as the grass.

Take kindly the counsel of the years, gracefully surrendering the things of youth.

Nurture strength of spirit to shield you in sudden misfortune. But do not distress yourself with dark imaginings. Many fears are born of fatigue and loneliness.

Beyond a wholesome discipline, be gentle with yourself. You are a child of the universe no less than the trees and the stars; you have a right to be here.

And whether or not it is clear to you, no doubt the universe is unfolding as it should. Therefore, be at peace with God, whatever you conceive Him to be. And whatever your labors and aspirations, in the noisy confusion of life, keep peace in your soul. With all its sham, drudgery and broken dreams, it is still a beautiful world. Be cheerful. Strive to be happy.

by Max Ehrmann© 1927.